Getting the Message

A READING COURSE FOR SCHOOLS

Dermot Murphy & Janelle Cooper

STUDENT'S BOOK

TWO

CAMBRIDGE
UNIVERSITY PRESS

Introduction

To the student

Welcome to Book Two of *Getting the Message*. Like the other books in this course it contains a variety of things for you to read; there are tasks to show you how to read more effectively and how to get more out of what you read. This section explains how this book is organised.

Remember that you learn to read by reading. It takes time and practice to learn a language, so do lots of reading. The more you read, the more you enjoy reading.

Unit layout

Phase	Exercise	Purpose
Before you read	1 TOPIC	To get you thinking about relevant ideas; to identify what you know about the topic; to check you know some relevant vocabulary.
	2 TEXT	To get you to use knowledge about the kind of text (text-type); to use information from pictures, diagrams, headings, the title; to help you to predict.

Phase	Exercise	Purpose
While you read	3 PURPOSE – FIRST READING	To give you reasons for reading so you know what to look for before you read and choose the appropriate reading style; later you will create your own purposes.
	4 CHECKING UNDERSTANDING – SECOND READING	To give you other ways, as you read the text again, to help you get at the meaning or organisation of the text, and interpret what is there.

Phase	Exercise	Purpose
After you read	**5** LOOKING AT LANGUAGE	To help you understand some of the vocabulary for the topic, and aspects of the grammar or structure for the text-type.
	6 THE TOPIC AND YOU	To use the reading you have done, combining the new ideas with others you had already. Good readers use their reading!

Phase	Exercise	Purpose
How you read	**7** DEVELOPING SKILLS	To help you to reflect on how you read and learn; to help you to develop fluency and confidence as a reader of English; to help you learn ways to get what you want from the text.

To the teacher

The three books in the course will help your students become good readers. There are various things for them to read about; there are different kinds of text; exercises to help them read more effectively, exercises to help them understand, and tasks where they use their ideas.

The **Overview** table on pages 4 and 5 shows you what is in each unit: what you will read, the topic of the text and the focus of the tasks. The **Unit layout** above shows you the steps which form the basis of the units. It will be useful to discuss each phase and exercise with your class; make sure they understand the purpose of each step, and make notes on these. At the back of the book you will find a **Skills profile** which sets out the things they need to know and do in order to become good readers. In each unit the final section gets you to discuss skills that the students have used.

You will find a detailed explanation of the ideas underlying this course in the accompanying **Teacher's Book**. This also contains suggestions on how to use the book in class and gives model answers to the exercises.

We hope that you enjoy *Getting the Message*.

Overview of Book Two

LANGUAGE	TASK	SKILLS
adverbials, word classes, word families	description	identifying the text type, opinion
simple vs continuous tense, compound nouns	story telling	reading for gist, prediction
definitions, *too* & *very*	poster display	scanning, skimming, giving an opinion
collocations, relative clauses	description of dress	deducing vocabulary, comprehension & reading purpose
word discrimination, word fields, conjunctions	search for information, a display	reading speed, intensive reading
matching word and definition	writing advice	coping with new vocabulary
word puzzle	analysing, writing advertisements	comprehension & reading purpose
reference and connectives	writing a questionnaire / making a poster	organisation & connection of ideas in a text
connotation	narrative / presentation on heroes	noting new phrases, identifying the text-type, opinion
synonymous words & phrases	presenting explanations	review of the skills being learned

Space Explorers
– part one

Before you read

1 TOPIC

Look at these newspaper headlines. What are the stories about? Work in a small group.

Mining Mess Angers Farmers

DAMAGE TO FARMLAND

Price of Gold Takes Off

SCIENTISTS WARN EARTH IN DANGER

Are you concerned about the Earth? Why? How are people spoiling the Earth? How can we look after our planet?

2 TEXT

Look at the pictures: how can you tell this is science fiction?

While you read

3 PURPOSE – FIRST READING

This is an episode from a story in *Sci-Fi Adventure* magazine. Look at these questions and then read the story and look at the pictures to find the answers.

1 How did the Explorers get to the planet?
2 What does the planet look like?
3 Why do the Explorers want to mine for metals?
4 How can you tell the Azzakians from the Explorers?
5 Why don't the Azzakians want the mines?
6 How can you tell the fence is dangerous?
7 Why do the Azzakians tell the Explorers to go?
8 Why do the Explorers call the Azzakians "Zaks"?

Did you answer all the questions? Compare your answers with a partner.

4 CHECKING UNDERSTANDING
– SECOND READING

Read these statements about the Explorers and the Azzakians. Which ones are true and which are false? Write correct versions of the false sentences.

1 The Explorers wanted to make mines for the Azzakians.
2 The Explorers wanted to mine for metals because they wanted to be rich.
3 The Explorers did not want to mine in the mountains.
4 The Explorers put up the laser fence to protect the Azzakians.
5 The Explorers thought the Azzakians were not dangerous because they had no army.
6 There are not as many Azzakians as there are people on Earth.
7 The Azzakians grow crops and keep animals in the mountains.
8 The Azzakians were angry because the Explorers caused trouble.
9 The Azzakians wanted to help the Explorers with food and land.
10 The Azzakians did not understand the warning signs.

After you read

5 LOOKING AT LANGUAGE

a) **Here is an entry from a diary kept by Lara, one of the Explorers. When did these things happen? Choose words from the table to fill the gaps, and write the complete entry.**

WEDNESDAY 6 AUGUST 2194

.... WE EXPLORED THE FARMLAND; WE HAD EXCELLENT RESULTS. THEN

.... WE TALKED TO THE ZAKS: THEY DON'T WANT US TO MINE HERE,

BUT UP IN THE MOUNTAINS! WE NEED THE GOOD METALS .... BECAUSE

WE'RE GOING TO BUILD THE SPACE STATION ON MARS .... FRANK SAYS

.... WE'LL BE RICH, THEN WE CAN GO AND LIVE ON EARTH AGAIN.

in (a, two, three etc.)	year(s) day(s)	this	year week
now today/tonight tomorrow		next	morning afternoon evening

Now write Lara's diary entry for Thursday.

b) Look at this sentence from the story:

Mining is difficult there.

Here *mining* is used like a noun. Which *-ing* words in the text are used like nouns?

c) Word families: how many words can you find in the text to go with *mining* and *farming*? Make two lists.

6 THE TOPIC AND YOU

What is Azzaka like? Now work in pairs: compare Azzaka and Earth. Use your imagination! Make a map of the mountains, countryside and farmland in Azzaka. Write short descriptions to show where things are: for example, where do the Explorers want to mine? Where do the cattle graze in summer and in winter? Where do the Azzakians grow crops? Name the city. Put in as many details as you can think of.

How you read ## 7 DEVELOPING SKILLS

Discuss these questions with your teacher.

1 You knew this was a science fiction story: how did knowing this help you? What did you expect the story to be like?
2 How did you use the title and illustrations to help you? How can they help you to understand the story?
3 What is your opinion of the story?

Space Explorers
– part two

1 TOPIC

Answer these questions on your own:
What do you think happened next on Azzaka?
What did the Explorers do?
What did the Azzakians do?
Make a note of your ideas and then discuss them with a partner.

2 TEXT

Do you ever wish stories had a different ending? The ending to this story now depends on the choices you make. You are one of the Explorers, and it is the day after the Azzakians died on the laser fence. Read on to find out what happens. Then start again, change your choices and see what happens. Have fun!

3 PURPOSE – FIRST READING

Warning! Do not read this story from beginning to end. Every time you come to a question, choose what to read next. Your choice will decide what happens to you. Will you be alive or dead at the end?

§188

A noise wakes you up. "Get up" says the loudspeaker. "We need everyone to guard the fence."

You get up with the other Explorers and go outside the guard house. It is early morning. There is a large number of Azzakians beside the fence. You have never seen so many of them before and they are making a lot of noise. While you are talking with the other Explorers, the sky begins to get dark. Astor says, "Let's go before they attack us," but Tel says, "No. Let's wait and talk to them."

★ What will you do?
★ If you decide to go, read **§195**
★ If you decide to stay, read **§192**

§189

You and Astor prepare the spaceship for take-off. Mirja orders Astor to start the engines and the ship lifts slowly into the atmosphere. Suddenly she shouts, "Our speed is too low. We won't get away. Increase the power." "But that's too

dangerous,' cries Astor. Mirja pulls the switch and the ship starts to move faster, then . . . You only see the flash, you never hear the bang. In the explosion Mirja, Astor and you become ashes.

§190

You walk over to Lara. "I can't move," she says. "It's difficult to breathe." "I know," you say, "I think the gravity is changing. Give me your hand." You take her hand and try to pull her up. She doesn't move. You try again and fall over. Unable to get up, you look around.

★ What do you see?
★ If people are on the spaceship, read **§193**
★ If the other Explorers are talking to the Azzakians, read **§194**

§191

The sky is black now. You can't see anything outside. Mirja turns on a light and you look for the others. They are still lying on the ground outside, and no one

is moving. "We can't leave them," you say. "If you go out," says Astor, "you won't come back with us." "You must decide now," says Mirja.

★ What will you do?
★ If you stay on board the ship, read **§189**
★ If you decide to go out, read **§190**

§192

Tel calls to one of the Azzakians, "Get your leaders. We'll talk." While you are waiting, you all argue about what to do. When the leaders arrive, they say, "Turn off the fence if you want to talk." Frank answers "But then we'll have no protection." You turn to him and shout, "Shut up! Look how dark it is, something's happening."

★ What do you decide?
★ If you want to turn off the fence, read **§194**
★ If you refuse to turn it off, read **§197**

§193

"Lara! Look at the ship," you say. "Can you see?" "Yes!" The lights inside are on, and you can see Mirja and Astor at the door. They shine a light towards you. "We're here!" you both call. They turn the light off and close the door. You feel sick. "Don't leave us!" cries Lara. "Don't leave us!" After some time the engines start, and then the ship moves. It lifts into the atmosphere, very slowly. You look at Lara. "The gravity . . . " she says quietly. The engines roar louder, lifting away from you. You cover your ears. Boom! The explosion shakes the ground. In its light you see Frank and Tel on the ground to your right, you see the fence and the city. You are on Azzaka for ever.

§194

You see that Tel and the others are talking to the Azzakians. They agree to turn off the fence. The Azzakians cross the line, join hands and sing in low voices. The sky begins to get lighter.

"How did you do this?" you ask an Azzakian. "We love our planet; we talk to its spirit and it helps us," she answers. "Take your machines to the ship," one of the Azzakians orders. You all start to work and take things to the spaceship. The Azzakians watch. The spaceship is ready and the Azzakians cheer when you close the door. That's the last you see of the planet. Tel starts the engines for the long journey home.

§195

You start to run towards the spaceship, but it is difficult. The sky is darker and you feel heavier, as if gravity is changing. You stop to get your breath back. While you are resting, you see Lara trip and fall. She shouts, "I can't get up. Help me!"
★ What will you do?
★ If you go to help her, read §190
★ If you continue walking to the ship, read §196

§196

You finally reach the spaceship and climb in. The sky is very dark now. You see some of the other Explorers lying on the ground, trying to get up but unable to stand. In the cabin, Astor and Mirja are preparing for take-off. "Let's go right now," says Astor. "Don't wait for the others. It's too late for them."
★ What do you do?
★ If you decide to take off now, read §189
★ If you decide to wait, read §191

§197

"What are you doing?" you ask the Azzakians. One of their leaders replies, "We can't let you destroy our planet. We have a duty to Az, the spirit of Azzaka, to protect this planet. We don't have your weapons but we have older ways. Turn the fence off, please." Frank cries, "They'll kill us. Let's go." And he pushes you out of his way.
★ What do you do?
★ If you go, read §195
★ If you stay and talk more, read §194

4 CHECKING UNDERSTANDING – SECOND READING

Answer as many questions as you can on your own.

1 When did the sky begin to get dark?
2 Why did Mirja turn on the light?
3 When did you see Lara trip?
4 Why didn't Frank want to turn off the laser fence?
5 What was happening when you woke up?
6 What happened after Mirja increased the power?
7 When did the gravity begin to change?
8 Why didn't Astor and Mirja want to wait?
9 How did the Azzakians protect their planet?
10 Why did you feel sick?
11 Why couldn't Lara move?
12 How much do you like each Explorer? Put them in order – including yourself!

Now, in a group of three or four, compare your lists for question 12, and see if together you can answer all the questions.

After you read # 5 LOOKING AT LANGUAGE

a) **Look at the two forms of the verbs in these sentences. Why are they different?**

While you were talking with the Explorers, the sky began to get dark.
While you were resting, you saw Lara trip and fall.

b) **Now read this story about a strange happening and put the verbs in brackets into the correct form.**

Louis was a Space Explorer. One day, while he (*work*) in an asteroid mine, a strange thing (*happen*) to him. He had taken the landing shuttle and left the mother ship. He (*go*) down into the mine; as usual, he (*wear*) his spacesuit and helmet with a mining lamp. Suddenly he (*hear*) Freda calling him on the radio: "Come back to the ship quickly." While he (*fly*) back to the mother ship, he (*see*) a smaller asteroid hit the asteroid where they (*mine*). Both (*break*) into many pieces. He called Freda, "Did you see that? Wow, am I glad you (*call*) me!" Freda said, "I'm very glad you're safe, but who called you? It wasn't me."

c) **Some names of things are made up of two words: *spacesuit, laser weapon, gold mine*. Which is the main word? The first or the second? Is it always that word?**

The other word tells us:
WHERE
   A spaceship is a ship that is used in space.
What's a spacesuit?
WHAT IT CONTAINS
   A laser weapon is a weapon with a laser in it.
What's a laser fence?
WHAT IT'S FOR
   A gold mine is a mine where you find gold.
What's a diamond mine?

Which group do these words belong to?

science fiction   space station   asteroid mines   farmland
adventure story   mining lamp   space explorers
warning signs   guard house

6 THE TOPIC AND YOU

Now write your own story about a strange happening, or write what happens after §193.

How you read # 7 DEVELOPING SKILLS

Discuss these questions with your teacher.

1 Have you met this type of text before? How would you describe it? Did you like choosing your way through the story?

2 How much do you expect to understand when you read a story? Was this different?

3 What did you know about the topic? How did that help you?

All sorts of things

Before you read **1** TOPIC

Here's a questionnaire. Ask three people in your class the questions and write their replies.

Names			
Do you collect things?			
What do you collect?			
Do you talk to other collectors?			
How do you get new things for your collection?			

How many people in your class are collectors? What do they collect?

2 TEXT

Look at this text but don't read it yet. Who do you think wrote it? What do the illustrations suggest to you?

While you read **3** PURPOSE – FIRST READING

Here is an article from Clapham High School magazine, which the students write. Look at these questions first.

    1 What is a swap-shop?
    2 How old are the clothes on the German doll?
    3 Why does the coin collector find coins interesting?
    4 Where can you see the old Town Hall?
    5 Which stamps are very expensive?
    6 Which collection do you think is interesting?

Now read the article to find the answers.

ALL SORTS OF THINGS

Do you know that there's a Collectors' Club in the school? This term we asked them what they do, and they told us about some of their collections.

The Club

We meet on Thursday after school and have different groups. The biggest one is the stamp collectors; then the coin collectors; after that there are all sorts of things: toy cars, matchboxes, key-rings, insects, postcards, dolls. Sometimes people show us their collection and tell us why it is special. At other times we have a swap-shop, and people exchange duplicates, or swap something they don't want for something new. That can be fun because most people like bargaining. I bet you collect something — not just bad marks for homework — so you too could join the Club. Some of our keenest collectors are going to tell you about their hobbies.

Dolls

I started collecting dolls when my aunt gave me a china doll. It's the oldest one I have, it was made in Germany a hundred years ago and it still has its original dress and boots. It has beautiful hair. I'm going to buy another old one when I have enough money. My other dolls are modern. I have twenty-three. However, they're all different: they're made of plastic, wood and cloth. The smallest is 2cm tall. The most beautiful ones are from Italy and Spain, and they are dressed in regional costume. I also have a lovely wooden one from Japan. You could come and see them all at our Club.

Postcards

I have hundreds of postcards and they are all fascinating. I started collecting all sorts, from all over the world. That got too complicated, so now I only collect local ones. They are a history of our town during the last hundred years. One shows a tram in the High Street; another shows the old Town Hall, which was pulled down in 1951. The funniest thing is the clothes people wore. That's what I collect. You could collect foreign postcards or funny postcards.

Coins

Do you have some coins on you? One of them could be rare, and worth a lot of money. I found my rarest coin, a 1932 Florin, in some change. It's not the oldest one I have, that's a penny from 1797. I collect coins because I like the history they record. It's exciting to think how old they are. I am starting to collect coins from different countries, all made in 1936. How do I get them? I swap with my friends at the Club, sell some and buy some. I like learning about them in my catalogue. It's a very interesting hobby.

Stamps

Collecting stamps is great; I think they're the best thing to collect. There are so many different ones, from every country. Collectors usually have a theme: stamps from one country, stamps about space, animals, famous people etc. You could think of lots more. My theme is flowers. Collecting could cost you a lot of money, if you bought very old stamps. However, collecting modern stamps isn't too expensive. Anyway, the Club helps. I don't buy many stamps, I get mine by swapping with friends. It's good fun. Stamps look nice and a good album is beautiful. Come to the Club and I'll show you mine.

There are all sorts of things that you can collect. You must be interested in one of them. Why don't you come to the next meeting, and you could get the collecting bug?

Could you answer all the questions?

4 CHECKING UNDERSTANDING – SECOND READING

Copy the table about the four collections. Put a tick (✔) to show which ones include old items, modern items, items from different countries, or items linked by a theme. Write in what the special item is in any collection. Put *0* if you don't know; put a cross (✗) if there aren't any items.

Collection	Old	Modern	Different countries	Theme	Special item
Dolls	✔				

After you read

5 LOOKING AT LANGUAGE

a) Do we say *too* or *very*? Look at these examples. When do we use *too*?

> *This stamp isn't beautiful, why are you going to buy it?*
> *Because it's very rare.*
> *That doll is beautiful, why aren't you going to buy it?*
> *Because it is too expensive.*

Work with a partner and answer these questions.

1 These are good cars, why don't you want them?
Because they are .... old for my collection.
2 That stamp's really old. Why does Miriam like it?
Because it's .... beautiful.
3 Why don't you want that insect?
Because it's .... difficult to keep.
4 Why doesn't she want that coin for her collection?
It's .... new. She only collects old ones.
5 Did he really swap two cars for that postcard?
Yes, because it's .... funny.
6 He has all sorts of things. Why don't you like his collection?
I think it's .... big.
7 I like this key-ring. Why don't you want it?
Because it's .... big to put in my pocket.
8 I think this stamp's ugly. Why does Joan like it?
Because it's .... rare.
9 Do you want this matchbox?
No, it's .... dirty to swap for this.
10 Why does Mark think this doll is special?
Because it's .... old.

b) These are definitions of words in the article. Find the words in the word search; they have been printed across, up, down and diagonally. The first one has been done for you.

1 a group of people who meet for a common interest. (c ....)
2 to bring various things together (c ....)
3 to give one thing for another (s ....)
4 small piece of paper you put on a letter (s ....)
5 common subject, idea or interest ....)
6 amusing; makes you laugh
7 book for keeping cards, photographs etc. in
8 lists things (e.g. books) and records age, size, worth etc.
9 of or from another country
10 of or from one place

6 THE TOPIC AND YOU

Are you crazy about collecting? Do you have the collecting bug?

a) **Yes? Draw and describe some of the things you collect or would like to collect. Make a poster to show your class.**

b) **No? Make a poster about another hobby to show your class.**

How you read ## 7 DEVELOPING SKILLS

Discuss these questions with your teacher.

1 How did you read when you were looking for a specific piece of information, for example, a particular word?
2 How did you read when you wanted an impression of what is in the text?
3 What did you think of the collectors' ideas?

Fashion

1 TOPIC

What sort of clothes do you like to wear? Do your parents like them? What sort of clothes do your parents wear? Do you like their clothes? What clothes would you like to buy? Why?

2 TEXT

Look at the text. It comes from a computer in a museum and it is for visitors to read. What is each section called? Look at the first section: how do you choose what to read? Why does a museum present a text on a computer?

3 PURPOSE – FIRST READING

Look at the following questions.

  1 What is the topic of each screen?
  2 Where will you go first if you are interested in:
      jewellery?
      punk clothes?
      wigs?
      teenage fashion?
      the fashion industry?
      embroidery?
  3 How many different things are changed by fashion?

Museum of Fashion

HARD DISC

Introduction
Entrance hall

Welcome to the Museum of Fashion! This exhibition is all about clothes, shoes and hairstyles in Europe. It shows you what people have worn over the last five centuries. Each room has a different theme, and you can visit the rooms in any order. We hope that you will enjoy your visit, and learn from it as well. You may go away with some new ideas for what to wear!

This computer program tells you about the various displays, and where to find them. There is a computer in each room, which will tell you more about the theme of that room. Choose what to read next from the menu at the bottom of the screen.

Go to next screen

Being fashionable   Dressing to shock
Hairstyles   Introduction   Kids' gear
Men's fashions   Women's fashions

Rubbish

Museum of Fashion

HARD DISC

Being fashionable
Room one, ground floor

Every fashion goes through three stages. At first it is different; it may be new and exciting, shocking or surprising. Then it becomes popular, and the original idea is imitated. Finally it becomes boring and out of date as a new fashion starts.

Being fashionable says something about you. It means that you know what is smart, and suggests that you are up to date in other ways. Here we look at the reasons why people want to be fashionable.

Some changes in clothes have been practical, and reflect the different way that we live. But fashion is about having fun, and being up to date. Today fashion is a big industry, so we tell you about all the different people who work in it.

Go to next screen

Dressing to shock   Hairstyles   Introduction
Kids' gear   Men's fashions   Women's fashions

Rubbish

Museum of Fashion

Dressing to shock
Room five, first floor

When fashions shock, it is usually more than clothes that are changing. In the 1920s people were shocked when women cut their hair short, and wore short skirts. But, at this time, more women were beginning to work outside the home, and they had also won the right to vote. People were shocked when women started to wear trousers to work in the early 1970s, a time when women were demanding the same rights as men.

Later in the 1970s, many young people shocked and frightened the older generation. Their jeans were torn, they wore several earrings, put chains on their jackets, and had spiky, coloured hair. They were seen as rude and aggressive, and a few of them were, so for many people the clothes meant "here is an ugly, rude person". They were the punks.

Go to next screen

Being fashionable   Hairstyles   Introduction
Kids' gear   Men's fashions   Women's fashions

Rubbish

Museum of Fashion

Hairstyles
Room two, ground floor

Hairstyles, like clothes, follow fashion. Many past fashions were not practical and showed that the people who wore them were wealthy, and did not have to work. Hair can be worn short or long, it can be coloured, it can be plaited or worn in a bun. You can curl it, if it's not naturally curly, or you can cover it with a wig.

Every gentleman in the eighteenth century wore a wig. The gentlemen's servants also wore wigs, but people like farm-workers didn't. There is a large collection of wigs for you to look at, including some modern ones.

Go to next screen

Being fashionable   Dressing to shock
Introduction   Kids' gear   Men's fashions
Women's fashions

Rubbish

Museum of Fashion

HARD DISC

Kids' gear
Room four, first floor

This room displays the clothes which well-dressed children and teenagers have worn in the twentieth century. At the beginning of the century, very young girls and boys all wore dresses, and had long, sometimes curly, hair. Teenagers dressed like adults.

The big change started in the late 1950s when teenagers adopted blue jeans and t-shirts. A whole range of clothes was made for young people in the 1960s and after. Fashion became colourful and exciting, changed fast, and was designed for young people.

In the early 1990s many adults copied the bright tracksuits and trainers their children wore. But there are new ways to say, "I'm young!" You can see them here . . .

Go to next screen

Being fashionable   Dressing to shock
Hairstyles   Introduction   Men's fashions
Women's fashions

Rubbish

Museum of Fashion

HARD DISC

Men's fashions
Room three, ground floor

Men's clothes have changed a lot. In the sixteenth century, gentlemen's clothes were brightly coloured, and the cloth was patterned, and embroidered.

In the seventeenth century a wealthy man had silver buckles on his shoes, and lace at the end of his sleeves. He could be fashionable because he was rich.

However, not every fashion started with the wealthy. Trousers were worn by working men in the eighteenth century, but, by the beginning of the nineteenth century, they were also worn by fashionable men.

This display ends with the dark suit, and patterned tie men wear now.

Go to next screen

Being fashionable   Dressing to shock
Hairstyles   Introduction   Kids' gear
Women's fashions

Rubbish

File Edit Block Tag **Special CD**   3:33:47 PM

Museum of Fashion

HARD
DISC

Women's fashions
Room six, first floor

Before the twentieth century, European women wore
long skirts or dresses. Looking at these dresses, we notice
that there is a lot of beautiful embroidery, lace, and
decorative work including gold thread and pearls.

After the First World War, women's fashions changed
much more than men's. In the 1920s in Europe many
young women began to wear shorter skirts and very
short hair. Since Dior launched the New Look in 1947,
women's fashion has continued to change rapidly.

Look for the display of jewellery, with its large collection
of earrings.

Go to **next screen**

Being fashionable   Dressing to shock
Hairstyles   Kids' gear   Introduction
Men's fashions   Women's fashions

Rubbish

4 CHECKING UNDERSTANDING
– SECOND READING

a) Work on your own. Draw a floor plan for the museum;
you will have to invent some things e.g. where doors
are. Label each room with its name and things you can
find in there.

b) Work in pairs. Using information from the screens,
write your definition of "a fashion".

c) Work in a group of three or four. Write an advertisement
for the museum to go in a magazine which you read; use
between 15 and 25 words.

After you read

5 LOOKING AT LANGUAGE

a) Which words from the text can you put with these
words? Make three examples for each.

   fashion   hair   clothes   t-shirt   jeans

   Example: *a brightly coloured t-shirt, curly hair*

b) Imagine you have been to the museum. Complete these descriptions of things which you saw; there are two examples to help you.

I laughed at the .... which ....
I laughed at the wigs which the gentlemen wore.
I liked the .... which ....
I hated the .... which ....
I wish I had the .... which ....
I wish I had the jeans which were embroidered.
My friend wanted the .... which ....

6 THE TOPIC AND YOU

Draw a picture of yourself in your favourite clothes. Label your hair, clothes and shoes. Compare pictures in a group of three or four; tell the others which clothes shock your parents.

How you read

7 DEVELOPING SKILLS

Discuss these questions with your teacher.

1 What did you do when you met new words in the text? Don't just guess their meanings. Use clues to help you understand:
   What kind of word is it?
   Given the topic (fashion), what sort of meaning do you expect?
   Do you need to understand it better? Yes, then look in your dictionary or ask your teacher.
2 How much of the text did you need to understand for your purpose? Understanding every word is about learning vocabulary, reading is about understanding those words you need for your purpose.
3 What new things have you learned from reading the text?

Discoveries in medicine

1 TOPIC

Work in a group of three or four. Look at these messages.

Who puts up posters and notices like these? Why do they put them up? Where might you see them? Can you think of another message like these?

2 TEXT

This chapter is from a book on social history. Look at the pictures. What do you think this chapter is about? How many main ideas do you expect to find in the chapter?

3 PURPOSE – FIRST READING

Look at the following questions.

1 Why do people want to be healthy?
2 What did Empedocles believe caused malaria?
3 How were bacteria discovered?
4 How did Pasteur show that some bacteria were harmful?
5 How were operations made safe?
6 Why does the fight continue?

Now read the text to find the answers.

Chapter V   Medicine and Good Health

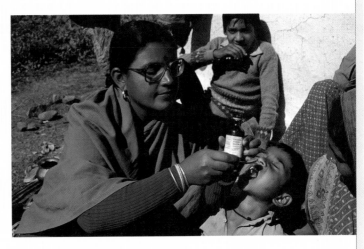

There are many things that we do not know about the history of medicine. For instance, how did it start? Who was the first doctor? We will never really know the answers to these questions. However, the purpose of medicine has always been the same, to cure disease and keep people healthy. It is important for society that people are healthy, so a lot of money is spent on hospitals and medicine. Healthy people have better, longer lives.

Money is also spent to help doctors and other scientists try to discover new ways to treat disease, and to explain why people are healthy and why they get ill. How do people catch a cold? Why do new diseases such as AIDS appear? The scientists do not know, but they can look for answers. The story of medicine tells us about finding answers and the scientists who found them. Often they had to change people's beliefs about health and about how their bodies work. In order to treat or prevent disease, people had to understand the world in new ways. Look at these cases.

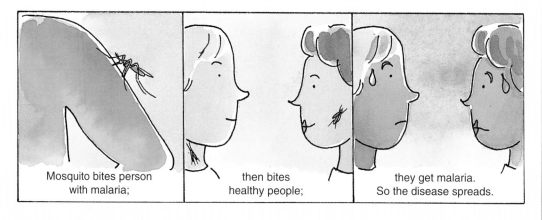

Mosquito bites person with malaria;

then bites healthy people;

they get malaria. So the disease spreads.

Bad air and mosquitoes

Once malaria was a more common disease than it is today, and many people died from it. The disease was found in more places than it is now, and some land was not farmed because malaria killed anyone who went to live there. For centuries people in Europe believed that the disease was caused by "mal aria" – "bad air". In the 6th century BC Empedocles wanted to protect the people of Selinus, in Sicily, from malaria; so he emptied the nearby marshes from which the "bad air" was coming. In this case the action was successful, but not because the air changed.

Empedocles' plan worked because there was no water in the marshes for mosquitoes to live in. Doctors in India knew in the 5th century AD that mosquitoes carry malaria, but European doctors only learned this at the end of the nineteenth century. In the seventeenth century they learned from the Incas in Peru to use quinine to treat the disease; but they still could not prevent people getting it. In 1955 the World Health Organisation (WHO) wanted to stop people getting the disease; so it planned to empty marshes and kill malaria mosquitoes all over the world. The plan worked very successfully, but now cases of malaria are increasing again.

Finding the invisible demons

Five hundred years ago many other diseases were common in European cities. Often a disease killed thousands of people at a time, as in the Great Plague of London in 1665. At that time doctors did not understand what caused diseases. It was believed that demons and bad air caused illness; or that people's bad actions made them ill.

A few years later, in 1674, a Dutchman, Leeuwenhoek, made a very powerful microscope and saw "hundreds of thousands of animals" that were living in the air, in water, and in his mouth! People could

Antony van Leeuwenhoek (1632-1723)

Louis Pasteur, (1822-95)

now see bacteria, but they did not understand that some of them, germs, were harmful. It was a French chemist, Louis Pasteur, who showed this, and that bacteria and germs live and grow, in fact, they are organisms like other animals. His experiments showed that living bacteria make food go bad, and that bacteria travel through the air.

In the nineteenth century surgeons were doing new operations, but many patients died after their operation because of "hospital disease". A surgeon in Scotland, Lister, read about Pasteur's experiments. He thought that if germs made food go bad then they could also make cuts go bad, so surgeons needed to kill the germs while they operated. Lister tried this and his patients did not get "hospital disease". In 1867 he told other surgeons how to prevent the disease with antiseptic surgery, but many did not believe him.

In 1867 cities in Europe were still unhealthy places where many people died from cholera and typhus. Pasteur's new ideas about germs explained why the diseases were common, so ways of stopping the germs from spreading were needed. Sewers were built to take away the dirty water where bacteria lived, and a supply of clean, pure water for drinking was organised. After that life in the cities changed and became much healthier.

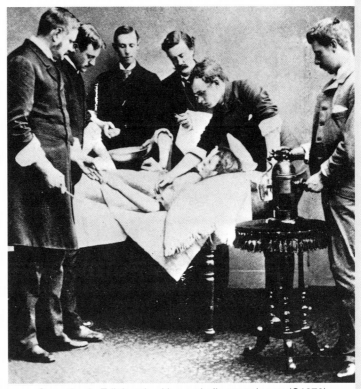

Operation in Edinburgh with a carbolic spray in use (C1870)

The fight continues

People like Leeuwenhoek, Lister and Pasteur changed our ideas and beliefs about disease, because they found the invisible demons, and how they work. Today, malaria, cholera and typhus are not as common, thanks to them. Through the World Health Organisation, countries work together to fight these and other diseases. However, it is a difficult and expensive fight. In most countries people live longer now, but everywhere diseases still kill.

Where people live in poor conditions without clean water or sewers, a disease can reappear, and kill again. This happened in the early 1990s, when cholera spread in parts of South America. Also, the bacteria can fight back; malaria bacteria have changed, and now resist scientific medicine, so that the disease has become more difficult to treat, and is spreading again. These examples show that the fight against disease is going to be a long one. Scientists must look for more answers and new ways to keep us all healthy, and this is expensive. So, although modern society spends a great deal of money on medicine, it has to decide whether to spend more, even if this will not stop disease completely.

4 CHECKING UNDERSTANDING
– SECOND READING

a) **Check your reading speed this time. See Exercise 7.1.**

b) **Read the following sentences. Which ones are true and which are false?**

1 Doctors do not understand why there are new diseases in the world.
2 A lot of money is spent on keeping us all healthy.
3 For centuries Europeans died of diseases caused by bad air.
4 Indian doctors knew before European doctors that mosquitoes carry malaria.
5 In 1665 the doctors gave scientific explanations for the Great Plague.
6 A Dutchman discovered that we have bacteria in our mouths.
7 Lister used Pasteur's ideas to make operations safer.
8 People built sewers in cities so that bacteria could live in them.
9 Scientists have changed our ideas about where diseases come from.
10 Society won't spend more money because diseases can't be stopped.

Now write correct versions of the false sentences.

c) **Lister met Pasteur in 1892, when Pasteur was an old man. What questions do you think Lister asked him? Write five questions, then ask someone else your questions. The answers do not have to be true.**

Examples: *Did you ever think that bad air made people ill?*
Do we spend enough money on medicine?
Are you going to do more experiments now?

Here are some ideas to help you: microscope; bacteria and disease; stop diseases; air; bacteria change; hospital disease; keep people healthy; change ideas.

After you read # 5 LOOKING AT LANGUAGE

Work on your own.

a) **Find the names of six diseases in the text.**

b) **Match these sentences:**

We prevented them from getting malaria.	They got better.
We treated them for malaria.	They didn't get malaria.
We cured their malaria.	They got medicine.

c) Find words in the text to fill the gaps.

Organism is to ...., as .... is to chemist, and as disease is to ....

d) Use one of these words or phrases to fill the gaps in the following sentences: *because, so that, why.*

1 People want to be healthy .... they have better lives.
2 Doctors are not sure .... new diseases appear.
3 Malaria was common in Europe .... people didn't kill mosquitoes.
4 Pasteur explained .... food went bad.
5 Sewers were built .... cities became healthier places.
6 Malaria is a problem again .... the bacteria have changed.

6 THE TOPIC AND YOU

Work in a group of three or four.

a) Find out about other famous people in medicine e.g. Marie Curie, Elizabeth Blackwell, Alexander Fleming, or a famous doctor from your country. When did they live? Why are they famous? Use this and the information from the text to make a display. Show your display to the other groups.

b) Make a display about a doctor's work. What different things do doctors do? Where? When? Why?

7 DEVELOPING SKILLS

Discuss these questions with your teacher.

1 What was your reading speed for this passage? (927 words, target speed between 4.5 and 6 minutes.) Make a note of this so you can compare it with your speed in your first language, and in later units.
2 How did you read a text which has a lot of new information? Skim the whole text first and then read carefully.
3 Did you find some ideas difficult? When this happens, don't go back: skim ahead and then go back.

Can we help you?

Before you read

1 TOPIC

What sort of problems do people of your age have? Who do you ask for help and advice? Do you always ask someone you know? Is the advice useful?

2 TEXT

Look at the first text. It's part of a problem page in a magazine for teenagers. How can you tell this? What else do you expect to find on the page?

While you read

3 PURPOSE – FIRST READING

Look at these pictures. What problems do they suggest to you?

Now read the letters and match the pictures to the correct letter.

Work in pairs and compare your answers; discuss possible solutions to the problems.

This is Dulcie Butler's page for those of you with problems. If you want advice about something difficult in your life, then write to Dulcie. It can be a big problem or a small one; Dulcie will have some advice for you.

NO FREE TIME

Last Thursday my friends had a spare ticket for a pop concert. They asked me to go with them and the ticket was free. But I couldn't go because I had to look after my 11 year old sister. My father is a sailor so he's not at home and my mother works in the evenings. I asked Mum and she said no. I know she has to work but it's not fair that I have to look after my sister all the time. I can't ever go out with my friends except at weekends. What can I do?
From A L

NO PRIVACY

I am 15 and I have to share a room with my sister, who is 9. She is very untidy and I have to clean up her mess as well as keep my own things tidy. She never leaves my things alone and keeps opening the drawers of my cupboard and looking at everything. Nothing of mine is private. And I'm not allowed to do what I want. Mum says I mustn't listen to my radio at night because the noise keeps my sister awake. What can I do?
From B K

BIGGER BOYS

I have a problem at school. There's a gang of boys who go around together, and they pick on smaller and younger kids, including me. They often take my pens and pencils and the money I have for my bus fare home. If I don't give it to them, they say they'll hit me. They threaten the other kids too. Everyone knows that they are bullies but we can't stop them. Help!
From C W

NOT A FOOTBALL HERO

I am a boy of 16 and I'm very unhappy. I'm good at my schoolwork but not very good at sport. The other kids in my class laugh at me. I wear glasses and am the smallest boy in the class. I'm very short and thin and I don't have any muscles. I'm not popular with the girls either. My mother says that I shouldn't worry and that I'm just a late developer, but I am worried.
What should I do?
From D S

62

4 CHECKING UNDERSTANDING – SECOND READING

a) **Here is Dulcie Butler's advice to the letter writers. Match her answer with the letter. Notice that there are only three answers.**

A

It can't be easy sharing a room with an inquisitive little 9 year old. I think she's old enough to tidy her own things. I think you and your mother should show her how to put her things away tidily. Perhaps you could get a box with a lock and key so that you can lock your very special things away. If your radio is of the right type and if you have enough money, you could buy some headphones for it. Then your little sister won't be disturbed at night. But remember that when little sisters grow up, they can become good friends to their older sisters.

B

Your mother is right. You needn't be so unhappy. People develop at different rates. When I was 12, I was the tallest in my class and that made me unhappy. By the time I was 15 there were several others taller than me. I think you should take up a sport for which you don't need to be big. Forget football but how about surfing or cycling or long distance running? The more you use your muscles, the bigger they will become. And don't worry about the girls. Not every girl is attracted to big muscles.

C

It's not easy for your mother to be on her own and to have to work. She must also know that it is not easy for you and your sister. I'm sure she appreciates your help. I don't think you should be angry with your mother. Is there a neighbour who could look after your sister sometimes? Why don't you ask your mother? If not, then next time there's a concert during the week, perhaps you could take your sister with you. I'm sure she enjoys pop music too.

b) **Which answers are reported here?**

1 She suggested that I should take up a sport and then told me not to worry.
2 She advised me not to get angry and suggested that we should ask the neighbours for help.
3 She advised me to teach my sister how to tidy up and she suggested that I should lock my own things up. She also suggested to me that I should buy some headphones.

5 LOOKING AT LANGUAGE

Here are some dictionary definitions. Match the definitions to words in the letters and answers.

Example: Letter AL – (adjective) extra; not in use but there if needed
Answer: *spare*

1 Letter AL – (noun) a person who works at sea; any person who sails
2 Letter AL – (preposition) but not; not including
3 Letter BK – (verb) to use or to have with other people
4 Letter BK – (noun) dirty, untidy state; things out of order
5 Letter BK – (noun) sound, especially an unpleasant or unmusical one
6 Letter CW – (verb) to choose someone to treat badly or roughly
7 Letter CW – (preposition) opposite of 2
8 Letter CW – (verb) to show the intention to cause hurt or pain to others, especially if they do not obey/do what they are told
9 Letter DS – (noun) part of the body which connects two bones and shortens to move arms, legs etc.
10 Answer A – (adjective) too interested in other people's things
11 Answer A – (verb) to stop or upset the calm, peace or rest of
12 Answer B – (verb) to be pleasing to
13 Answer C – (verb) to feel thankful for, to be grateful for
14 Answer C – (noun) person who lives in the next house to, or not far from, oneself

6 THE TOPIC AND YOU

a) Write an answer to CW's letter. Give it to other people in the class: do they agree with your advice?

b) Write a letter to the magazine about a problem of your own (real or imaginary!). Then exchange letters with a partner and write the answer to your partner's problem letter.

How you read ## 7 DEVELOPING SKILLS

Discuss these questions with your teacher.

1 Which new words did you understand as you read the text? This means you have understood the sense, but may not be able to translate the word.
2 Which words didn't you understand? Did you need them to understand the text? If you didn't, ignore them. If you did, then how did you find the meanings?
3 Are you putting useful new words into your vocabulary book? How do you group them? Alphabetically? By family (words about the same topic)? As you meet them? With a translation? Or a picture? In a phrase?

If a star used it, would you buy it?

Before you read **1** TOPIC

Work in pairs to complete this questionnaire.

SWORF Marketing

Please answer the following questions in our market survey.

1 What advertisements have you seen in the last month?	a) b) c)	
2 Where did you see them? (in the street, in a newspaper or magazine, at the cinema, on television)	a) b) c)	
3 Which of these products does your family buy?	a) b) c)	
4 Did your family buy one of these products because of the advertisement?	a) YES NO b) YES NO c) YES NO	
5 What did you notice in these advertisements?	a) picture YES NO b) famous person YES NO c) humour YES NO	

Compare your answers in a group of three or four.

2 TEXT

This text is a magazine article that includes other texts: advertisements. Look at the advertisements first. They all want you to buy their product. How do they try to persuade you? Can you think of similar advertisements that you know?

Find out about these topics in the article. First, in which paragraph do you read about them? Secondly, what does the article say about them?

- famous people
- honesty
- promise of happiness

- for and against advertisements
- product placement
- something for everyone, or just for a few

IF A STAR USED IT, WOULD YOU BUY IT?

MAYLEEN DEAKIN ON ADVERTISEMENTS

IF YOU SAW an actor eating a Choco Bar, would you buy one? Last year, when everyone saw Gabriel Hopps eat one in the film *Run Into Trouble*, people bought lots more Choco Bars than before. Was that an advertisement? Well, the makers of Choco Bars paid a lot of money to have Gabriel eat one of their bars and not some other brand. It is a new way to advertise, called 'product placement'; the advertising people like it because we don't see it as an advertisement. After all, their job is to get us to buy things. How do they persuade us?

One way is to get someone famous to say they use or like a product. Choco Bars used a

film-star, Dentacreme uses a pop-star, Samia. The slogan in the advertisement is a line from one of her songs, so when you hear the song you think of Dentacreme. There is a message in all advertisements, and in this one it is: if you bought their product you would use the same toothpaste as Samia, a beautiful, exciting pop-star. So, if you cleaned your teeth with Dentacreme you would have a smile like hers, and be beautiful and exciting too. Samia knows about pop-songs, but does she know more about toothpaste than you do?

32   YOUNG HERALD

Some advertisements use an expert, someone who knows about the product, and someone we recognise. In the Tube Bikes advertisement we see Sean Elliott, the champion cyclist. This time the message is, he knows about bicycles, you can trust him, so buy a Tube Bike and become a champion too. Well, you have to remember that Tube pay him to ride their bikes: he would still be a champion if he went to work for Penworth Cycles next year.

You don't have to be famous to be in an advertisement. Some ads are saying 'everybody likes this, you must like it too'. Look at the Dorcobon ad for their clothes for young people. The slogan doesn't say much, but you know it means 'if you had clothes like all of us, you'd be smart too'. However, they show that you can have clothes like everybody else and be in fashion, but wear your own colours. They know you don't want a uniform.

Other advertisers know that you don't want to be like everybody else. You want something that is just for a few people. Like Spike trainers. You probably don't have any because they are so expensive, and the advertisement wants you to think they are special. Even if you had the money, you wouldn't be sure of getting a pair. So anyone wearing Spikes is special.

Do you want friends? Do you want a good-looking girl or boy to love you? Some advertisements use romance to persuade you, like Stratton jeans, and many cigarette companies. If you wore Stratton jeans, they suggest, somebody would love you. Other advertisements use a different kind of love. The Holland cakes advertisement talks about your grandmother, who loves you and keeps all the family happy by buying Holland cakes. It is not romance, but the message is that Holland cakes will make you and everyone else happy. In other words, these advertisements say that you can buy happiness.

You probably buy sweets, and want them to taste good. So Jefferson's tell you their taste is special. It is different from the taste of other sweets. Is it? If you didn't see the bag would you know that you had a Jefferson's sweet? The message in the Jefferson advertisement is not very modest, but Constructo's tries to be. 'You will like us because we don't say we are the best.' They want us to notice their message because it looks more truthful.

However, the simplest message of all is 'Buy!', like the advertisement for Samia's new record. They just tell us the product is there, they don't tell us anything else about it, and they don't try to persuade us. It's only because she is a well-known pop-star that the advertisers can use such a simple message. In this case there is no hidden message. Because advertisers use hidden messages, some people don't like advertisements. These people think that advertisers persuade us to buy things we don't want, and that it isn't necessary to advertise. A few advertisements are not true, for example some medicines do not do what the message says. However, most ads are honest, and they tell us about new products. Also, the money from advertising pays for television programmes, and if newspapers had no advertisements they would cost more. Many people say that they do not believe the messages, anyway, and that advertisements do not influence them. What do you think? Write and tell me what you think about advertising, and I'll publish the best letters on this page.

4 CHECKING UNDERSTANDING – SECOND READING

Classify the advertisements by message. Identify the main message, and if the advertisement makes use of more than one message, then put that too. Make a list of the advertisements in the text and put the appropriate letters after each one.
Example: *Dentacreme (a) (f)*
Does the advertisement say the product:

a) is used by famous people?
b) is used by experts?
c) means that the buyer is special?
d) means that the buyers are like their friends?
e) is better than similar products?
f) will bring the buyer something extra e.g. love, beauty etc.?

5 LOOKING AT LANGUAGE

Can you find words in the article to match the meanings given here? The answers are given but the letters in each word have been jumbled.
Example: *a set of two things – arip = pair*

1 A sign or notice that tells people about a product. *trameedivents*
2 A particular product, or its name. *drnab*
3 Person who knows a lot about something. *teperx*
4 Working trousers made of denim. *sanej*
5 Point made by a book, article etc. *smaseeg*
6 Make person believe or think something. *rudesepa*
7 Person or thing many people like. *proalup*
8 Thing made by person or machine. *drupcot*
9 Of a particular sort, not like others. *acelips*
10 Product for cleaning teeth. *ashpototet*

6 THE TOPIC AND YOU

a) **Look at the advertisements which your teacher gives you; classify them like the advertisements in Exercise 4. Cut the advertisements out and put them in your exercise book. Write what you think the message is. Are there other messages? Do any of them ask if you are afraid? Like this one:** *Can't do your homework? Wouldn't it be easier if you had Knowledge magazine?* **Or the Stratton advertisement, which says** *Are you afraid nobody will love you?*

b) **For fun: think of a product, for example, a homework machine, or a shoe-cleaning machine. Draw it and write an advertisement for it.**

7 DEVELOPING SKILLS

Discuss these questions with your teacher.

1 How much of the text did you need to understand for your purpose?
2 Are you understanding enough of the text for your purpose? If not, discuss your difficulties with your teacher.
3 Are you understanding more quickly? If so, do you know what things have helped you to improve?

Do you  your heart?

1 TOPIC

Why would doctors put these notices up in their surgeries?

Which one is in danger of a
heart attack?

You can't tell, but you can prevent heart trouble. Ask your doctor, or pick up a leaflet.

Which of these foods are good for you?

Don't know?
Pick up a leaflet to find out.

When did you last get some excercise?

The fat aren't old and the old aren't fat.

TAKE A LEAFLET
to find out how to
exercise and live longer.

2 TEXT

Look at the leaflet on page 46. Where do you think you would find it? Who do you think produces it? Who should read it?

3 PURPOSE – FIRST READING

Look at the posters in Exercise 1 again.

a) What three things do they want you to learn about?
b) What information do you need in order to understand these things? Write down three or four questions. For example, why is some food bad for you? Then read the text.

DO YOU  YOUR HEART?

How to keep fit, eat well and avoid heart disease

I thought you couldn't have a heart attack if you were eighteen. And I used to play football; I thought I was fit.

It was so sudden. I came home from school, and my mum was crying. Dad had had a heart attack at work. They'd taken him to hospital.

You may be young and active, but this leaflet is for you. It's never too soon to start looking after your heart.

Did you know that heart disease can start when you're a child?

Did you know that up to 30% of people die of heart disease?

Do you know what you can do to avoid heart disease?

What are **you** doing to show that you love your heart?

This leaflet will help you to answer these questions.

♥ WHAT IS HEART DISEASE?

In fact there are several heart diseases. This leaflet tells you about the disease that causes a heart attack. It is the commonest type, and is called coronary heart disease. The disease is caused by things which we can control.

How does your heart work?

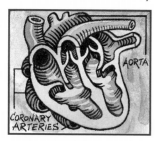

Your heart is about the same size as your fist, and is like a bag made of muscle. About 70 times a minute the muscle contracts to pump blood around the body. The heart muscle needs a good supply of oxygen and gets this from blood vessels, known as coronary arteries. These arteries branch off from the main artery, called the aorta, and then divide right and left into smaller branches which go all over the surface of the heart. Your heart works all day and night, but it rests between contractions. It likes exercise as all muscles do.

2

How does it start to go wrong?

Over a period of time, your arteries may get hard, or may get narrow because fat is deposited on the inside. Gradually the heart gets covered in fat, too. These changes reduce the blood supply to the heart, so the heart muscle itself gets less blood to make it work. Then you have coronary heart disease.

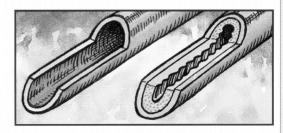

What happens then?

When the arteries get too narrow or get blocked, the heart has to work harder than it did before, particularly when you make an effort, for example, when you go upstairs. The first signs of trouble may only be noticed when the heart is having to work much harder like this. You get angry or run for a bus, and suddenly feel a heavy pain across the chest, which usually lasts only a short time. This kind of pain is known as angina. The other symptom of coronary heart disease – a heart attack – happens when a coronary artery is blocked. In this case, part of your heart stops working. The blockage may be so serious that the heart stops working completely, and, unless the heart starts beating again within a few minutes, you will die. When the blockage is not as serious as this, you will feel a severe pain which can last for several hours.

Which people get heart disease?

Heart disease affects men more than women. In some countries, like the United Kingdom, 30% of people under 75 die of heart disease but in other countries, like Japan, the percentage is very much lower. However, it is increasing in these countries because people are changing the way that they live.

♥ YOUR HEART AND THE WAY YOU LIVE

How likely are *you* to have heart disease?
What can *you* do to look after your heart?
We know that many things cause coronary heart disease, and you can control some of the important ones by what you do – and don't do. Check if you are doing the right things for your heart.

Do you smoke?

All my friends at school smoked. My dad smoked; he didn't want me to smoke but my friends kept saying I was stupid. They asked when I was going to grow up. So I

3

started. I was sixteen and after a month I couldn't stop. But two years later I could feel what smoking was doing to me. I couldn't run far, and I coughed every morning. I got very ill and decided to stop. It wasn't easy, but now I've done it, I feel better. And I have the money for other things.

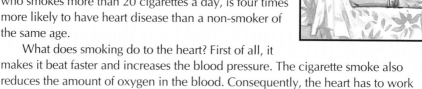

If you smoke, you are twice as likely to die from a heart attack. And the more you smoke, the earlier the heart attack is likely to be. For example, a 50-year-old who smokes more than 20 cigarettes a day, is four times more likely to have heart disease than a non-smoker of the same age.

What does smoking do to the heart? First of all, it makes it beat faster and increases the blood pressure. The cigarette smoke also reduces the amount of oxygen in the blood. Consequently, the heart has to work harder, with less oxygen. Finally, your arteries will narrow faster if you smoke.

So if you want to reduce your chances of getting heart disease, the answer is easy – don't smoke. Don't copy your friends and other people who smoke. If you smoke, find out how to stop. Stopping isn't easy, but you'll be healthier, and you'll have money for other things.

What do you eat?

Another way of reducing your chances of getting heart disease is to watch the types of food you eat. Certain foods produce the fat which is deposited in your arteries, and eating too much of these kinds of foods is the main reason for people being overweight. The best way of reducing your weight is to cut down on the amount of fat and sugar you eat.

* Cut the fatty bits off meat; eat more chicken, fish, fruit and vegetables.
* Grill, boil or steam food rather than fry it.
* Cut down on dairy products: butter, cheese and cream.
* Don't eat so many cakes, pastries, sweets and chocolate.
* Don't drink colas or sodas which have sugar in.
* Eat foods which contain fibre: wholemeal bread, fruit and vegetables.

A year ago, my father was told his blood pressure was too high. Since then, we've changed the food we eat. I didn't like it at first, but I do now. We have more fruit and vegetables, and very little fat. We've cut out sugar and salt. We make lots of new dishes, and my father says he feels very fit and healthy. So do I!

4

Do you take any exercise?

Any exercise is good for your heart – from athletics to yoga. There is good evidence that these activities can help you look after your heart. Like any other muscle, the heart gets stronger with use. The exercise needs to be regular and frequent – once a year is not enough! And the more vigorous the exercise is, the better it is for you. Swimming hard is better for you than a walk in the park, but that is better than watching television. It's a good idea to start a sport now that you can continue after you leave school.

    Look after your heart and it will look after you!

Published by Morella Area Health Authority

Check your answers to the questions from Exercise 3.

4 CHECKING UNDERSTANDING – SECOND READING

a) **Choose the correct word from one of the pairs to complete the sentences.**

less/more   increase/reduce   cause/prevent

1 If you don't smoke, you're .... likely to get a heart attack than a smoker.
2 Smoking .... your chances of getting heart disease.
3 Not smoking can help .... heart disease.
4 To be healthy, you should .... the amount of fat that you eat.
5 One way to do this is to eat .... fried food.
6 Being overweight may .... heart disease.
7 Eat .... fruit to .... heart disease.
8 Stop smoking, ... your chances of heart disease and get .... out of life!

b) **Put a tick (✔) against the foods that you should eat more of and a cross (✗) against those you should eat less of.**

bananas	*biscuits*	*carrots*	*dairy products*
fried potatoes	*jam*	*ice cream*	*nuts*
Choco Bars	*apples*	*cake*	*sweets or candy*

5 LOOKING AT LANGUAGE

Work in pairs.

a) **Find all the uses of *this* and *these* in the text. What does each use refer back to? For example, in the sentence *This leaflet will help you to answer these questions* on page 46, *these questions* refers to the four preceding questions.**

b) **A writer shows the connections between ideas in a text. Certain words are used to do this; e.g. *and* adds one idea to another.**

> *It is the commonest type **and** is called coronary heart disease.*

Other connecting words used in this text include:

> *because   but   consequently   however   so so . . . that*

Look back at the uses.

> Which of these words shows that one thing is the cause of another?
> Which of these words shows that one thing is the result of another?
> Which of these words contrasts two ideas?

6 THE TOPIC AND YOU

a) **Work in a group of three or four. Write a questionnaire to find out how much the students in another class know about heart disease, good diet, and keeping fit.**

b) **Work in pairs to make a poster to put up in your class:**

> "A plan for a healthy heart".

7 DEVELOPING SKILLS

Discuss these questions with your teacher.

1 How are the different ideas organised in the text? What is done to help you follow the ideas?
2 How do the connecting words help you to understand the argument in the text?
3 Did you understand the reference to earlier ideas in the text?

A Popular Hero

1 TOPIC

Look at this dictionary definition:

hero ['hɪerəʊ] *n* **-oes heroine** ['herəʊɪn] *fem* **1** a person who is admired because they are brave, or good *Gandhi was the hero of India* **2** the main character in a book, play, film, etc.

heroic [hɪ'rəʊɪk] *adj* **1 a** showing the qualities of a HERO **b** showing bravery

Name two heroes from history. Why are they famous? Were they both good? How long ago did they live? How much do you know about them?

2 TEXT

Look at the two texts. The first is a note from a theatre programme for the play *A Popular Hero*, and the second is a scene from the play itself. List three things which are special about each text-type.

3 PURPOSE – FIRST READING

Before you read the programme note, look at these questions.

1 Where did Robin Hood and Ned Kelly come from?
2 When did they live?
3 What did they do with the money they stole?
4 What happened to them in the end?
5 How true are the stories about them?

Now read the note to find the answers.

POPULAR HEROES
IN THE POPULAR MEMORY

Most countries have stories about popular heroes who helped ordinary people. However, these heroes are not usually mentioned in history books. In England the popular hero is Robin Hood, who robbed the rich and gave the money to the poor. He and his gang of followers, including Maid Marion, Little John and Friar Tuck lived in a forest near the city of Nottingham. They were outlaws, which meant that they were not protected by the law, so that anyone could kill them. They attacked the unjust governor, who was very cruel to the poor citizens of Nottingham; the gang made him look stupid, and sometimes they killed a few of his men. Robin is remembered as a just man who did good: he was not greedy, he understood and helped poor people. However, that was a long time ago, in the early thirteenth century. Now nobody knows if he really lived, and the stories about him may not be true. Perhaps the message in the story is more important than the truth about the man.

The Australian popular hero is Ned Kelly. Ned, his brother Dan, Joe Byrne and Steve Hart were outlaws and lived in the outback, north of the city of Melbourne. For two years, 1878 to 1880, the gang was famous all over Australia. They killed three policemen who were hunting them, robbed two banks and also stole cattle from big farms; some of the money and some cattle were given to the poor. The police looked foolish because they could not find the four men. The gang hid in the bush; then, in June 1880, they went to Glenrowan where they fought the police. Ned was injured and taken by the police, but the other three were killed. The court found Ned guilty and he was hanged in Melbourne prison; he was twenty-five when he died. Songs have remembered him as a brave "hero who gave to the poor", and have called the Governor of Victoria "a most unpleasant man". We know that Kelly lived, but, as with Robin Hood, we cannot be sure all the stories about him are true. The stories are remembered for what they say about ordinary people fighting against the rich and powerful.

4 CHECKING UNDERSTANDING – SECOND READING

Compare the stories of Robin Hood and Ned Kelly. Make two lists showing the things they did, what happened to them, and what people say about them. Which things in your lists are the same for both men, and which are different?

While you read

5 PURPOSE – FIRST READING

Here is a scene from near the end of the play. Judge Barry of the Melbourne Court has said that Ned Kelly must hang for his crimes. Ned's sister, Kate Kelly, and his lawyer, David Gaunson, go to ask the Governor to let Ned live. Look at these questions first:

1 Who did not like hanging?
2 Did the lawyer think that Ned Kelly should go free?
3 How did the Governor describe Ned Kelly?
4 Why did the Governor support the police?
5 Where is Mrs Kelly?
6 Did Ned Kelly kill anyone in the banks he robbed?
7 Who supported Ned Kelly and why?

Now read the scene to find the answers.

Act 3 scene 3 *The office of the Governor of Victoria*

Governor: Good afternoon, Mr Gaunson. I hope your business is brief, I'm a busy man.

Gaunson: I know that, sir. May I introduce . . .

Governor: I think I know who this is.

Gaunson: Sir, Miss Kelly and I have come to talk to you about her brother. We would like to ask you to stop the hanging.

Governor: And spare a murderer's life? I know, Mr Gaunson, that you do not like hanging, but this man is the most dangerous criminal we've ever seen in the State of Victoria.

Kate: Have you thought why he did those things? My brother . . .

Governor: Miss Kelly, how old are you?

Kate: Eighteen.

Governor: At your age you should know that your brother is a bad man. He's guilty of murder and robbery. Anyway, I was speaking to Mr Gaunson.

Gaunson: As you know, sir, we've collected a petition. Sixty thousand people have given their support, and ask you not to hang Ned Kelly.

Kate: My brother hasn't always been an outlaw: he was an overseer on a farm in Mansfield.

Governor: Miss Kelly, must I remind you that he killed three policemen, he robbed the banks in Euroa and Jerilderie, he's admitted that he stole cattle and horses and he's terrified the people of two states? Those are serious crimes.

Kate: He didn't frighten the people of Greta. He hurt no one in Euroa or Jerilderie; the people in Glenrowan welcomed him.

Governor: Nonsense.

Kate: They did. And you know they did. Why couldn't your police find Ned? Because he has so many friends. Because we all looked after him. We hate your police. Our lives are difficult, but the police have made them impossible.

Gaunson: I think, sir, what Miss Kelly says is important. Let me put the case to you. The court has found Mr Kelly guilty. He must, therefore, be punished. He could go to prison, or be hanged. But there are two reasons for not hanging him.

Governor: And what are they?

84

Gaunson: The State says murder is a crime. But the State kills people: it hangs those found guilty of murder and it allows anyone to kill outlaws.

Kate: And people don't want you to kill Ned. They know he's good.

Gaunson: The State cannot be guilty of this crime, of hanging people, of killing Ned Kelly.

Governor: The State protects people who live by its laws. Those who break the law are punished. And Kelly's punishment is hanging. What's your second reason?

Gaunson: The first was general. The second is about poor people in this State, like Mr Kelly. They have hard lives. They struggle. And the police make life difficult for poor people like Ned Kelly. So he and others turn to crime in order to live.

Governor: I never thought that you would say something so stupid.

Kate: It's you who is stupid. The police have persecuted us for years. Why has our mother been in prison for two years? The policeman who put her in prison has left the service. He's the criminal. You made him leave because he was no good.

Gaunson: This is true. The police are weak and corrupt. They hurt innocent people . . .

Kate: My brother hurt nobody in Euroa or Jerilderie. He took the money for us, for poor farmers, not for himself. He robbed banks not people. He wants liberty and justice for the farmers. He's had the courage to fight, and they respect him for it.

Gaunson: As Miss Kelly's told you, the farmers support Mr Kelly.

Governor: Which farmers? Not the ones that I meet. And who supports a murderer?

Kate: My brother is not a murderer. Those police were going to kill Ned and his friends. They fought to protect themselves.

Gaunson: Sir, we cannot live in a State where some of the people are frightened of the police, where they have no justice.

Governor: Our police do a difficult job in a State where people are frightened of outlaws and murderers. I've listened to you for long enough.

Kate: Have you heard what we've been saying? Have you understood?

Governor: You must understand, Miss, that justice has to be done. That liberty comes through justice. Good day to you both.

85

6 CHECKING UNDERSTANDING
  – SECOND READING

Look at the scene again. Make four lists:

> *1* the arguments for and against hanging;
> *2* the arguments for and against hanging Ned Kelly.

Choose one of the arguments and write it out as a letter to the *Melbourne Herald*. Exchange letters with a partner, and read your partner's letter.

After you read # 7 LOOKING AT LANGUAGE

a) **The Governor calls Ned Kelly a criminal. Which other words in the play and programme note mean something similar to "criminal"? What is the difference between them and "criminal"? Use a dictionary to help you.**

b) **Kate says that Ned is "good"; the Governor says he is "bad". Which other adjectives are used to describe people in the texts? Group them as "good" or "bad".**

c) **Imagine that you are a reporter from the newspaper, *The Age*. You are going to interview the Governor after David Gaunson and Kate Kelly have taken the petition to him. Plan five questions to ask him. Then interview a partner who will answer as the Governor.**

8 THE TOPIC AND YOU

Work in a group to make a display about a popular person in your country: think of a woman or man who is famous. Why are they popular? When did they live? What did they do? Write a story about them. Are all the stories about them true? Did anyone not like them?

How you read # 9 DEVELOPING SKILLS

Discuss these questions with your teacher.

1 Which useful phrases from these texts, for example *It's you who is stupid*, have you noted down? Why did you choose them? How will you remember them?

2 Did you identify the text-types (see Exercise 2)? How did knowing the text-type help you to understand the texts?

3 What do you think of the play and the ideas it contains?

Unit 10

The Bermuda Triangle

Another Triangle Mystery

FISHERMAN SEES FLYING SAUCERS

Planes lost at sea

Search finds nothing

Before you read

1 TOPIC

These headlines refer to the same news story. What do you think happened and where? What is the mystery? Look at the illustrations because they may help you. Note down your ideas.

2 TEXT

This chapter is from a book called *Great Mysteries of Our Time*. On the back of the book it says: "Do you like mystery stories where strange and frightening events take place? Are there mysteries in real life? Do we know the cause of everything that happens to us or are there some things we cannot explain?" What do you predict you will find in this chapter? Make notes.

CHAPTER 7 *The Bermuda Triangle*

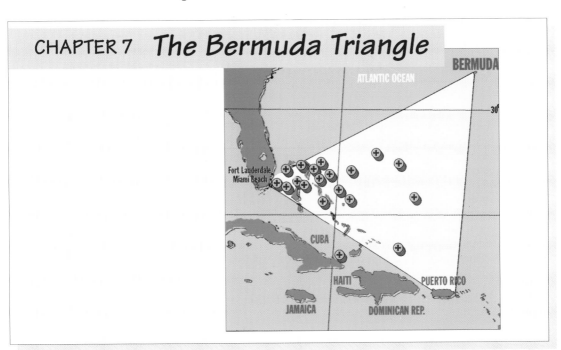

3 PURPOSE

Check your predictions from Exercises 1 and 2.

On 5th December 1945, Flight 19, which consisted of five US Navy planes took off from Fort Lauderdale in Florida in fine weather. There was a total of fourteen men on board the planes. The planes were in good condition, they had the best equipment including compasses and radios on board, and they also carried life-rafts. The planes could stay afloat on water for ninety seconds. One and a half hours after take-off, a radio message from one of the planes was heard at the control tower at Fort Lauderdale.

"I don't know where we are."

After that the planes could no longer speak to the control tower, but they could speak to and hear each other, and the control tower could hear them.

"The magnetic compass is going crazy."

"We're completely lost."

No other messages were heard after that. Nobody else heard from the planes or saw them again. Three hundred planes and many boats searched the area, but not one trace of Flight 19 was found. Then one of the planes that was sent to look for them also disappeared completely.

These planes had vanished in a very mysterious part of the world in the western Atlantic Ocean where lots of strange events have taken place. The mystery started long before 1945 and since that year, many other ships and planes have also disappeared in this area. It is called the *Bermuda Triangle*. As the map shows, it is a large, triangular part of the ocean with the island of Bermuda at its northern tip.

Planes and ships disappear in other parts of the world, but there are more disappearances in the Triangle than in other areas. For years now scientists and others have been puzzled by this mystery. There have been many attempts to explain why people, planes and ships vanish in such numbers here. Several books and many articles suggest theories which explain why travelling into the Triangle carries more risks than travelling in other places.

19

One writer, John Spencer, believes that the ships and planes have been carried off from the sea and sky by flying saucers or UFOs (unidentified flying objects) from another planet. Since there are millions of other planets in the universe, Spencer believes there must be other intelligent creatures somewhere in the universe. These creatures are interested in collecting humans and their equipment so that they can examine them carefully.

Some people believe that thousands of years ago there were very intelligent people on Earth who lived in places that are now under the sea. Their machines and the sources of power for the machines are believed to still be on the ocean floor. Another author suggests that these may sometimes start working again when planes fly overhead, thus causing the planes' magnetic and electronic equipment to stop working properly. The overflying planes therefore crash.

Another theory is that the geography of the area is responsible for the disappearances of the ships. Bermuda lies in an earthquake belt. Underwater earthquakes result in large waves, called tsunami, appearing suddenly. These waves are so big that they can break a ship in two, and spread its wreckage over a large area. In the air a similar thing can happen to aeroplanes because of sudden strong winds.

20

As with Flight 19, many boats and planes have reported that their magnetic compasses stop working properly in the Bermuda Triangle. Normally a magnetic compass points towards magnetic north. However, the Bermuda Triangle is one of two places on Earth in which a compass points towards true north. Therefore, there is something strange about the magnetic properties of the area. Some people have also suggested that the magnetic force is not stable in the Bermuda area and actually varies in strength. The magnetic variation could break a plane into pieces. So, according to this theory, if a plane enters a disturbed magnetic area, it will 'disappear'.

Many people have found these explanations difficult to believe and completely reject the idea of visitors from outer space. However, the most recent theory has a scientific basis and is more believable. The discovery of methane gas on the seafloor of the Bermuda Triangle started a scientist, Dr McIver, thinking about an explanation for the mysteries. Sometimes large amounts of the gas escape from the seafloor and rise into the air. This could produce large waves on the surface which would make a ship sink. When the gas mixes with air, it could also cause a ship's engine to stop or it could start a fire. Similarly, as the mixture rises into the air, it could cause an aircraft's engine to stop or to explode. The explosions would break a ship or a plane into tiny pieces.

This latest theory has yet to be proved but seems to offer a better explanation as to why Flight 19 and all the other planes, ships and people disappeared.

Were your predictions from Exercises 1 and 2 correct? Work in pairs to compare your ideas.

4 CHECKING UNDERSTANDING – SECOND READING

a) **Check your reading speed on this reading. (See Exercise 7)**

b) **Planes do crash, so what was unusual about the disappearance of Flight 19? Complete the left-hand column of these notes. Do not repeat any information.**

   Example:

   1 The weather was fine, but the planes disappeared.
   2 .... not one body was found.
   3 .... the compass stopped working.
   4 .... they couldn't speak to the control tower.
   5 .... not one was found.
   6 .... no part of the planes was found.

c) **Make notes on the explanations for the disappearances.**

   What is the THEORY: how did the planes/ships disappear?

   WHO or WHAT caused the disappearance?

   What ideas SUPPORT the explanation? (They may not be facts.)

   THEORY   WHO/WHAT   SUPPORT

5 LOOKING AT LANGUAGE

Often you will find two or more ways of saying the same thing in a text. At the beginning of the article, for example, you will find *mystery*, and then *strange and frightening events* and *some things we cannot explain*, which mean the same as *mystery*.

1 Find a word or phrase in the article which means the same as the following:

Flight 19   disappeared   flying saucers   tsunami not stable

2 Can you explain these in your own words?
compass   life-raft   humans   crash   wreckage

6 THE TOPIC AND YOU

a) **Can you think of any other explanations for the disappearances of the planes and ships? Set out your explanation and show it to your friends. Which explanation do you believe?**

b) **Describe another mystery from the Bermuda Triangle or somewhere else in the world. Write up what happened and give any explanations.**

7 DEVELOPING SKILLS

Discuss the questions in this section with your teacher. Monitor how you read. Talk to others about how you and they read.

1 Have you improved your reading speed? (This text is 820 words long. Target speed 4 to 5 minutes.) What is your speed now?
2 How much of the text could you understand? Was it enough for your purpose? What made the text difficult? How can you overcome these difficulties?
3 What helps you to understand more quickly?
4 How can you use the ideas from the Developing skills sections next time you read?

Skills profile

The **Developing skills** section in each unit refers to this table. There are four areas for you to develop. The advice is intended to guide you in developing as a reader and learner of English. Write notes in the comment column on your progress. You may do this in your first language.

Skills profile	Units	Comment
Reading style		
Adjust your reading speed to suit your purpose for reading and the type of text. However, reading faster helps you understand: don't slow down too much!		
1 Check your average reading speed: in your first language and in English. Keep a record.	5, 10	
2 When you look for a specific piece of information, scan. Look for the word by shape, first letter, capital letters.	3	
3 When you want an impression of what is in the text, skim. Read it quickly, looking at the title, headings, beginnings and endings of paragraphs to get a general idea.	Ex. 2 TEXT in each unit 3, 5	
4 When you want the main information or are reading a story for pleasure, read for gist. This means reading quickly, ignoring detail and understanding 60–70% of the text.	2	
5 When you read a text which has a lot of new information, skim to get an impression and then read it again more slowly. You can help yourself understand better by asking yourself questions and by making notes. Several quick readings will work better than one slow reading.	5	
Prepare, read, and check what you have understood.		

Language

	Units	Comment

Reading is a great way to build vocabulary and acquire grammar, and the more language you know, the better you will be able to read.

	Units
6 You can understand some new words because of the context.	6
7 If you don't understand some of the new words, ask yourself if you need them to understand the text.	6
8 If you do need a word, don't guess its meaning: use clues to help you understand: the kind of word it is, the topic, the ideas you expect. If you still need to understand it better, look in your dictionary or ask your teacher.	4
9 Put useful new words into your vocabulary book. Decide how to group them: alphabetically, by family (words about the same topic), as you meet them, with a translation, with a picture or in a phrase. Choose the method that suits the words and suits you.	6
10 Record new ways to say things (whole phrases or sentences).	9
11 Notice the ways to refer to earlier ideas, for example, words like *it*, *this*, *one*, and some uses of *do*.	8
12 Notice the ways to connect ideas, using words like *and*, *but*, *however*, *because*, *therefore*. These show different relationships between the ideas.	8
13 Ideas are organised in different ways; notice how one topic leads to another. If the text is well constructed, then this will help you understand the author's ideas.	8

Interpreting and understanding

Understanding what we read is complex. It comes from what we know about the topic, how much language we know, what we expect to find in the type of text, as well as adding to and changing these ideas and expectations with new reading.

Good readers use prediction to help them.

	Units
14 Use the title, illustrations, diagrams or headings to help you predict the content and the meanings. Ask yourself before you start reading what you know about the topic.	1, 2, 9

	Units	Comment

Know why you are reading the text.

15 Decide how much of the text you need to understand for your purpose. Understanding every word is about learning vocabulary, reading is about knowing which words you need to understand for your purpose.

Ex. 3
PURPOSE
in each
unit
4, 7, 10

16 If you find the ideas difficult, don't go back: skim ahead and then go back, if you need to. Talk to others about what you've read. Share the ideas and fun you get from reading.

17 Discuss your opinion of the story or of the ideas: what you liked and didn't like, or what you agree and what you disagree with.

1, 3, 9

18 Talk about any new ideas you have learned from the text or that have come to you from reading the text.

4

Learning reading skills

Monitor how you read. Talk to others about how you and they read.

19 Things you might ask about include: adapting your reading style to the text; improving your speed; ways of dealing with new language; how you get ideas from texts; what things you like reading.

7, 10

20 Keep notes in the Comment column so that you can see when you improve. Remember to use your reading skills whenever you want to get the message.